Holly's Book For Jesus

Holly Hamilton

O give thanks unto the LORD; for he is good; for

his mercy endureth for ever.

1 Chronicles 16:34 KJV

This book is dedicated to my Lord and Saviour Jesus Christ. I pray that my book will make God happy and help lead my family and friends to walk with Jesus and go to heaven.

Forward

By Lisa Hamilton

While I was writing my book, "His Legacy of Love", my daughter, Holly, informed me that she was ready to start writing hers. I thought it was very sweet that she wanted to follow her mommy and write a book as well. That was until we sat down and she gave me 10 chapter titles with ease! Then I knew it that it was a divine assignment. We are so blessed and thankful to our God who continues to lead us and overwhelm us with His great love and care for our family.

Introducing sweet Holly Hamilton and her new book,
"Holly's Book for Jesus"

God Saves Us From Sin

This is the very best gift God has given to us. If we follow Him we can live forever with Him in heaven.

For God so loved the world that He gave His only begotten Son,

that whoever believes in Him should not perish

but have everlasting life.

John 3:16 NKJV

Therefore if the Son makes you free,

you shall be free indeed.

John 8:36 NKJV

God Prays For Us

Jesus is closer than a brother and He will pray for us.

That they all may be one, as You, Father, *are* in Me, and I in

You; that they also may be one in Us, that the

world may believe that You sent Me.

John 17:21 NKJV

Now He is also able to save to the uttermost those who come to God through Him, since He always lives to make intercession for them.

Hebrews 7:25 NKJV

God Takes Us To Heaven

**We were created to walk with God
and live with him in heaven.**

In my Father's house are many mansions: if it were not so, I would have told you. I go to prepare a place for you. And if I go and prepare a place for you, I will come again, and receive you unto myself; that where I am, there ye may be also.

John 14:2-3 KJV

But Jesus said, "Let the little children come to Me, and do not forbid them; for such is the kingdom of heaven"

Matthew 19:14 NKJV

God Gives Us Animals For Friends

I am happy God created pets to be our friends.

These are my dogs King and Koa.

Your righteousness is like the mighty mountains, your justice like the ocean depths. You care for people and animals alike, O LORD. How precious is your unfailing love, O God! All humanity finds shelter in the shadow of your wings.

Psalm 36:6-7 NLT

The wolf also shall dwell with the lamb, The leopard shall lie down with the young goat, The calf and the young lion and the fatling together; And a little child shall lead them.

Isaiah 11:6 NKJV

God Gives Us A Heart To Love People

When we love and care for others
we make God happy.

Trust in the Lord with all thine heart; and lean not unto thine own understanding. In all thy ways acknowledge him, and he shall direct thy paths.

Proverbs 3:5-6 KJV

But the mercy of the Lord is from everlasting to everlasting On those who fear Him, And His righteousness to children's children.

Psalm 103:17 NKJV

God Gives Us Friends To Pray For Us

Thank you God for giving us friends to love us and pray for us.

Again I say to you that if two of you agree on earth

concerning anything that they ask, it will be

done for them by my Father in heaven.

Matthew 18:19 NKJV

This is My commandment, that you love one another

as I have loved you. Greater love has no one

than this, than to lay down one's

life for his friends.

John 15:12-13 NKJV

God Protects Us

When we walk with Jesus we have nothing to fear.

What then shall we say to these things? If God *is* for us, who can be against us?

Romans 8:31 NKJV

I look up to the mountains does my help come from there?

My help comes from the Lord, who made

heaven and earth!

Psalm 121 NET

God Gives Us Yummy and Healthy Food From The Garden

Thank you God for giving us so many good fruits and vegetables.

Then God said, "Look! I have given you every seed-bearing plant throughout the earth and all the fruit trees for your food.

Genesis 1:29 NLT

But he answered, "It is written, 'Man does not live by bread alone, but by every word that comes from the mouth of God.'"

Matthew 4:4 NET

God Gives Us A Family To Love

I love my big family. Thank you God!

Honor your father and your mother, and, You

shall love your neighbor as yourself.

Matthew 19:19 NKJV

Love is patient and kind. Love is not jealous or boastful or proud or rude. It does not demand its own way. It is not irritable, and it keeps no record of being wronged. It does not rejoice about injustice but rejoices whenever the truth wins out. Love never gives up, never loses faith, is always hopeful, and endures through every circumstance.

1 Corinthians 13:4-7 NLT

God=Jesus=Love

I love my God the most because He gave me His love!

And this is eternal life, that they may know You, the only true God, and Jesus Christ whom You have sent.

John 17:3 NKJV

For God is Love

1 John 4:8b NKJV

Thank you for reading my book. I hope you enjoyed it. God bless you!

Check out my mom's book available on Amazon and Createspace. For more Scripture, inspiration and testimonies please follow us on Facebook (happyinsing)

God has done amazing things for our family. In [illegible], at my conversion in Batam, Indonesia, He instantly healed me from lifelong anxiety and depression. God replaced that darkness with His love, purpose, and deep joy.

As I walk with Him on this awesome spiritual journey, He has revealed Himself in incredible ways with many beautiful encounters, healings, and miracles, including the documented miracle healing of our son, Michael, from fetal hydrops at the Lighthouse Church in Singapore.

We have experienced many trials, but God gave us victory and a beautiful testimony.

I pray that we can bring hope as we share the new life and the love that Jesus Christ has given to us, for God's glory!

Revelation 12:11 KJV

And they overcame him by the blood of the Lamb, and by the word of their testimony; and they loved not their lives unto the death.

Hebrews 13:8 KJV

Jesus Christ the same yesterday, and to day, and forever.

Barcode Area

We will add the barcode for you.

Made with Cover Creator

His Legacy of Love

Lisa Hamilton

His Legacy of Love

Lisa Hamilton

Made in USA - Crawfordsville, IN
27492_9781719060318
04.11.2020 0058